My Handprints
My Footprints

To my husband and children who are my greatest inspirations

Illustrations: Rebecca Shore, Jerusalem
Copyright to the text and art work: Gefen Publishing House, Ltd., Jerusalem
Typesetting and Graphics: Studio Tali and Dorit, Jerusalem

Text adapted in part from the original Mazal Tov book compiled by Masha Fridman,
Copyright: Gefen 1981
All illustrations are gouache and ink on strathmore paper
Text set in gentle sans

ISBN 965 229 178 1

Edition 9 8 7 6 5 4 3 2 1

Gefen Publishing House Ltd.
POB 36004, Jerusalem
91360 Israel

NORTH AMERICAN DISTRIBUTION:

Alef Judaica
8440 Warner Drive
Los Angeles, CA 90232

Printed in Israel

Baby's First Record Book

gefen גפן
publishing house בית הוצאה לאור
JERUSALEM ◆ NEW YORK

Illustrated by Rebecca Shore

...על כל הארץ ביום ההוא...

...over all the world, on that day...

Events Around the World

(paste newspaper clippings here)

(Zechariah 14:9) (זכריה י"ד, ט)

I was born on

Hebrew date *English date*

at

hospital *address*

The doctor who delivered me was

My birth certificate number is

My identification bracelet

The color of my eyes is

My hair color is

My weight at birth is

My length at birth is

These are my birthmarks:

welcome home
ברוכים הבאים

Today is _______________ _______________
day *date*

I came home with

My address is

I am wearing

The weather is

These people are here to greet me

Now that I'm home...

I asked my Father how he felt, and he said:

I asked my Mother how she felt, and she said:

This is my first week at home

This is how I am behaving

Feeding

Sleeping

(Exodus 7:25) (שמות ז, כ"ה)

עץ חיים היא
It is a tree of life...
Mother
Me
Sibling
Sibling
Family ancestry, yichus, has played an important role throughout Jewish history.
Enter names in each circle indicating the members of your family. You may also include birthplace and birth date.
Members of the Mother's family are recorded on the left side of the tree.
Members of the Father's family are recorded on the right side of the tree.

It is a tree of life... עֵץ חַיִּים הִיא
It is a tree of life... עֵץ חַיִּים הִיא
Father
Our Family Tree
Sibling
(Proverbs 13:18)
(משלי י"ג, י"ח)

As he has entered the covenant, so may he enter
a life of Torah, marriage and good deeds
And his name shall be called in Israel

Baby's English name son of _Father's English name_

The Brit Milah, the Covenant of Circumcision, is the induction of the Jewish male into the Jewish people. Traditionally, on the Friday evening before the Brit, guests are invited to a Shalom Zachor, to "welcome the little boy." On the eighth day following the baby's birth, friends and family gather to participate in the ceremony of the Brit Milah. The Mohel, specially qualified, performs the circumcision. The baby is held on the lap of the Sandek, who is seated on the decorated Chair of Elijah the Prophet, while the Mohel performs the small operation. Elijah the Prophet is known as the "Angel of the Covenant" and witnesses all circumcisions. After the circumcision, the baby is named and the guests remain for a Seudat Mitzvah, a festive meal, honoring the new child.

Place of circumcision ______ Date ______

Mohel ______

Sandek ______

(Genesis 12:17) (בראשית י״ב, י״ז)

כשם שנכנס לברית, כן יכנס לתורה, לחופה, ולמעשים טובים

ויקרא שמו בישראל

______________ בן ______________

Father's Hebrew name *Baby's Hebrew name*

Pidyon Haben

Redemption of the First-Born Son

קדש לי כל בכור פטר רחם בבני ישראל (שמות י״ח, ט״ז)

Consecrate every first-born child in Israel unto Me *(Exodus 18, 16)*

The Torah commands us to "Sanctify...all first-born sons of Israel." This commandment applies only to a first-born child who is male, and whose father or mother does not belong to a family of Kohanim or Levites. On the thirty-first day after the birth of the boy, the father "redeems" his son through the symbolic transaction of giving five silver shekels to the Kohen. The ceremony is followed by a festive meal.

Date ______________ Place ______________

Kohen ______________

He who has blessed our forefathers
Abraham, Isaac and Jacob, Sara, Rebecca,
Rachel and Leah, He will bless the Mother
and the daughter born to her. Mazal Tov.

מי שברך אבותינו
אברהם, יצחק ויעקב
שרה, רבקה, רחל ולאה
הוא יברך את האשה היולדת
ואת בתה הנולדה לה
במזל טוב!

The birth of a daughter is an occasion of rejoicing which centers around the naming of the child. Traditionally, the father is called up to the Torah in the synagogue. A prayer for the health of the mother and child is said, and the name is announced. At the gathering following the ceremony, friends and family greet the new baby and wish her a joyous future,"...to the canopy and to good deeds."

(Eichah 2:13) (איכה ב, י"ג)

ויקרא שמה בישראל

And her name shall be called in Israel ______

Daughter of ______

______

Baby's English name ______

Mother's English name ______

Mother's Hebrew name ______

______

Baby's Hebrew name ______

______

Synagogue ______

Date ______

Guests ______

______

______

(Shir HaShirim 3:11) (שיר השירים ג, י״א)

Breastfeeding: date ended

supplements

Comments on early feeding

Date

Bottle-feeding: formula

water

juice

milk

I drank my last bottle on

I start eating solids

First food

Second food

Third food

(Kings I 4:20) (מלכים א׳ ד, כ)

I drink from a cup

I drink from a cup without spilling

I can feed myself

I eat with the family

My favorite foods are

	Weight	Height
Birth		
1st week		
2nd week		
1 month		
2 months		
3 months		
4 months		
6 months		
8 months		
12 months		
18 months		
2 years		
3 years		

(Genesis 26:13) *(בראשית כ״ו, י״ג)*

ונשמרתם ... take care of yourself ...

My Health Record

My pediatrician is ________________

Examinations

Date	*Age*	*Findings*

Immunizations

Date	*Type*

Allergies ________________

take care of yourself... לנפשותיכם

(Deuteronomy 4:15) (דברים ד, ט״ו)

	Date	Age
I start teething		
I brush my teeth		
My first tooth falls out		
My first permanent tooth grows in		
My visits to the dentist		

MY TEETH

Give date when each new tooth appears

(Genesis 49:12) *(בראשית מ"ט, י"ב)*

My sleeping habits

My activity level

My concentration level

My temperament

My attitude towards others

I can eat by myself

I can wash myself

I can dress myself

My favorite activities

Songs

Stories

Records

Toys

Sayings

... but pleasant words are pure.

My Speech and Activity Record

Speech development is one of the most important phases in a child's growth.
Here is a chart recording my speech progress.

	Date	Age
I make cooing sounds		
I smile		
My first word: English		
Hebrew		
I say my name		
I give a kiss		
My first sentence is		
My first prayer is		
My first question is		
I can sing a song		

and he shall cut...his hair
:יְגַלַּח אֶת... שְׂעָרוֹ
MY FIRST HAIRCUT
It is the custom among many Jews to wait until after the third year to cut a child's hair. This tradition has its roots from the Torah where man is likened to "a tree of the field." The law requires one to allow a tree to grow its fruit for the first three years after planting. Only in the fourth year has the fruit achieved its maturity and can be eaten. The child, after his first phase of maturity, after three years, has his hair cut.
Here is a lock of my hair
Date of haircut
Cut by
(Leviticus 14:8)
(ויקרא י"ד, ח)

my FIRST birthday
Place
Date
My guests
My gifts
...and there was light, gladness, joy and honor...
(Megillah 8:16)
(מגילה ח, ט״ז)

For the sake of my brothers and friends
For the sake of my brothers and friends.
My Friends
My best friends are
The places we go
My friends are
I first slept over at
Our favorite activities
I spend my summer at
(Psalms 122:8)
(תהילים קכ"ב, ח)

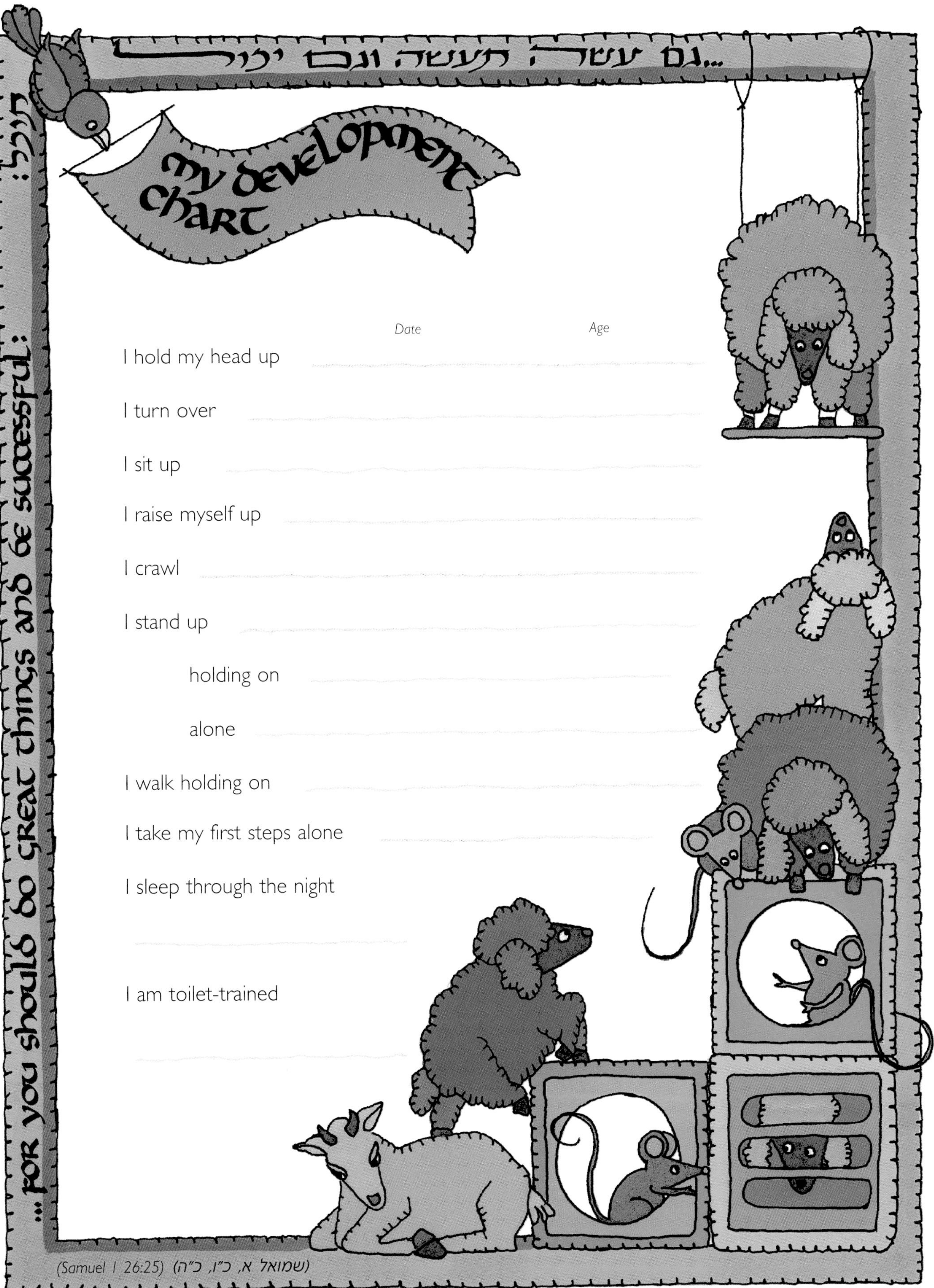

...גם עשה תעשה וגם יכל תוכל:
my development chart
Date
Age
I hold my head up
I turn over
I sit up
I raise myself up
I crawl
I stand up
holding on
alone
I walk holding on
I take my first steps alone
I sleep through the night
I am toilet-trained
...for you should do great things and be successful:
(Samuel I 26:25) (שמואל א, כ"ו, כ"ה)

...ועת לשחוק... ועת רקוד...עת לשמור
My Family vacations
Picnics
Beach
Zoo
Favorite trips
Our family occasions
...a time to laugh...a time to dance...a time to keep...
a time to laugh...a time to dance...a time to keep...
(Ecclesiastes 3:4/6)
(קהלת ג, ד/ו)

My First Trip to Israel
והיה כי תבוא אל הארץ...
and when you shall come to the land...
and when you shall come to the land...
והיה כי תבוא אל הארץ
Date
Places visited
My impressions
(Deuteronomy 26:1)) (דברים כ"ו, א)

ושננתם לבניך ודברת בם, בשבתך בביתך...

And you shall teach them to your children...

First Day in Nursery

I went to ______ nursery today ______
name of nursery *date*

My teacher's name is ______

My playmates are ______

These are things we do ______

First Day in School

I went to first grade today ______
date

The name of my school is ______

My teacher is ______

My classmates are ______

______

(Deuteronomy 6:7) *(דברים ו, ז)*

... and you shall write all of these things ...
כתב לך את כל הדברים אשר דברתי אליך...
A B C D E F G H I J K L M N
I can write a letter of the alphabet
I can write a letter of the Aleph-bet
I can write my name
O P Q R S T U
(Jeremiah 30:2)
(ירמיהו ל, ב)

The holidays are a time of awe and excitement for the child. The customs and preparations revolving around each holiday involve the Jewish child in unforgettable experiences. These include building the Succah on Succot; dancing with the Torah on Simchat Torah; lighting candles on Chanukah; dressing up for Purim and joining in the Seder on Pesach; and many others.

This is how I participate in each of the holidays.

... the wise of heart will accept the commandments...

חכם לב יקח מצות

(Proverbs 8:18) (משלי ח', י"ח)

Date

My first blessing

I light candles on Shabbat with my Mother

I say Kiddush with my Father

I say Shma Yisrael

I give money to charity

I visit my sick friends

I go to my first Brit Milah

I go to synagogue with my Father

(Deuteronomy 16:14) (דברים ט"ז, י"ד)

heed my child the command
ments of your father... תורת אמך
נצר בני אביך ואל תטש
My Bar/Bat Mitzvah!
12
13
11
4
5
10
1
8
6
7
2
3
9
Date
Torah Portion
Haftarah
Synagogue
Picture
(Proverbs 6:20)
(משלי ו, כ)

שמח תשמח רעים האהובים...
give abundant joy to these beloved companions...
abundant joy to these beloved companions...
MY MARRIAGE
My husband/wife
Synagogue
Date
Officiating Rabbi
Picture
(Tr. Ketubot 8a)
(מס' כתובות ח, א)

MY
BABY
place YOUR baby's picture here
(Psalms 106:31)
(תהילים ק"ו, ל"א)

My First Drawing